**Helping Children See Jesus**

ISBN: 978-1-64104-053-2

# God and Israel
*New Testament Volume 22:
Romans, Part Four*

Author: Marilyn P. Habecker
Illustrator: Frances H. Hertzler
Colorization courtesy of Good Life Ministries
Page Layout: Patricia Pope

© 2019 Bible Visuals International
PO Box 153, Akron, PA 17501-0153
Phone: (717) 859-1131
www.biblevisuals.org

All rights reserved. No part of this publication may be reproduced, stored in a retrieval system or transmitted in any form by any means, electronic, mechanical, photocopy, recording or otherwise, without the prior permission of the publisher, except as provided by USA copyright law.

## RELATED ITEMS

To access related items (such as activities, memory verse posters and translated texts) please visit our web store at www.biblevisuals.org and enter 1022 at the top right of the web page. You may need to reduce the zoom setting to get the search box.

## FREE TEXT DOWNLOAD

To obtain a FREE printable copy of the English teaching text (PDF format) under Product Format, please scroll down and select Extra–PDF Teacher Text Download. Then under Language select English before clicking the ADD TO CART button to place in your shopping cart. Other languages are available at an additional cost from the Language menu. When checking out, use coupon code XTACSV17 at checkout and click on Apply Coupon to receive the discount on the English text.

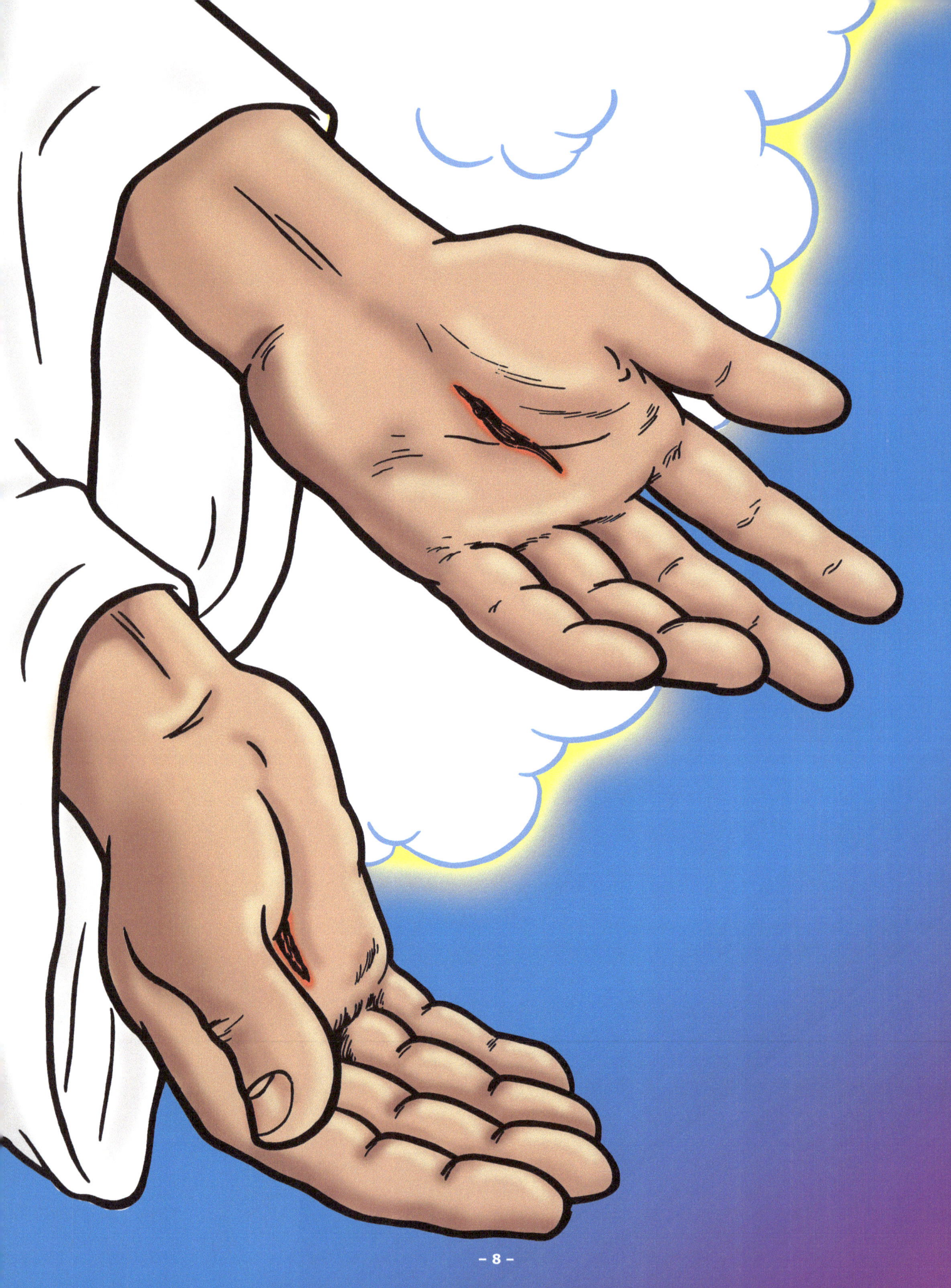

For whosoever shall call upon the name of the Lord shall be saved. — Romans 10:13

# Lesson 1
# GOD AND ISRAEL IN THE PAST

## NOTE TO THE TEACHER

The Righteousness of God is the theme of the book of Romans. (Have you observed how often the word "righteousness" appears in Romans?)

We have already seen that God is righteous in condemning sinners. He is righteous in justifying those who trust in His Son. And He is righteous in sanctifying (setting apart) His own people.

Again in chapters 9, 10 and 11 the Apostle Paul stresses the righteousness of God. These three chapters relate particularly to the nation of Israel–its past, present and future. They show that God is righteous in all His dealings with Israel.

It is important that your students understand that in the Bible the Jewish people are usually referred to as Israelites and Hebrews. Paul used each of these terms when speaking of himself. (See Acts 21:39; Romans 11:1; Philippians 3:5.) Jews are descended from Abraham.

If you live in a part of the world where there are few Jews, you may be tempted not to teach this volume. That would be a great pity, since so much of Bible history and prophecy (and today's news!) has to do with the Jewish people. Study carefully and pray earnestly that these lessons may be used to meet the needs of those you teach.

**Scripture to be studied:** Romans 9

**The *aim* of the lesson:** To show the blessings God gave to Israel because of His love for them.

**What your students should *know*:** Even though Israel refused to receive Jesus Christ, God still loves Israel and offers salvation to both the Jews and us.

**What your students should *feel*:** A desire to place their trust in the Lord Jesus.

**What your students should *do*:** Believe on the Lord Jesus Christ as Saviour and receive Him.

In the past, Israel (the Jewish people) received seven love gifts (blessings) from God (Romans 9).

**Lesson outline (for the teacher's and students' notebooks):**

1. God "adopted" Israel as a son (Exodus 4:22; Romans 9:4).
2. God's glory–His presence and power–were with Israel (Romans 9:4).
3. God made covenants (agreements) with Israel (Romans 9:4).
4. God gave His Law to Israel (Romans 9:4).
5. God gave the Israelites a special service of worship (Romans 9:4).
6. God gave the Israelites His promises (Romans 9:4).
7. God gave the Israelites fathers (ancestors) (Romans 9:5).

**The verse to be memorized:**

*For whosoever shall call upon the name of the Lord shall be saved.* (Romans 10:13)

## REVIEW

1. What is the book of Romans about? *(The righteousness of God)*
2. God is righteous in condemning the world. What does condemnation mean? *(To declare guilty of sin; to prove guilty of sin; and to pronounce the penalty for sin)*
3. How many have sinned? *(All)*
4. What is the punishment for sin? *(Eternal death–separation from God forever)*
5. What does justification mean? *(To declare righteous)*
6. How can God, the righteous One, declare righteous those who trust in His Son? *(He can declare them righteous because the Lord Jesus bore the penalty of sin on the cross and God now sees believers as being in His Son. Romans 3:21-26.)*
7. What does sanctification mean? *(To be set apart by God for God)*
8. How many people are sanctified? *(All who have their trust in Christ)*
9. When is a believer sanctified? *(The moment a person places his trust in the Saviour, God sets him apart for Himself.)*

## THE LESSON

Whatever God does is right, whether or not we understand what He does. It was so in the long ago. It is so today.

When the Apostle Paul wrote his letter to the Romans, he knew that some puzzled born–again Jews would read the letter. They were puzzled because they expected that God would do a great work among the Jewish people. (Jews are also known as Israelites and Hebrews.) But Paul had openly said that he was turning from preaching to the Jews to preaching to the Gentiles. (All people who are not Jews are Gentiles. See Acts 13:46.) Numbers of Gentiles had placed their trust in the Lord Jesus Christ and were no longer condemned. But most of the Jews turned their backs on Him and opposed the Gospel message.

The Jews knew that God had chosen them for Himself. They expected that He would first bless them in particular ways. Instead, the Gentiles were the ones being blessed. And the Jews could not understand it.

In Romans 9, 10 and 11, Paul shows that God was righteous in the past when He chose Israel as His treasured people; He is righteous in whatever He does with Israel in the present; and He will be righteous in what He does with Israel in the future.

In your notebook, please write:

**A. God and Israel in the Past**
Romans 9
Israel Elected

Write also the entire memory verse for this volume–Romans 10:13. It is important to remember that whoever (whether Jew or Gentile) calls on the name of the Lord Jesus Christ and trusts in Him, will be saved. It is equally important to remember that no one (whether Jew or Gentile) can be saved any other way than by trusting in the Lord Jesus Christ.

Today we study the past history of Israel as given in the ninth chapter of Romans. Early in the chapter Paul reveals that he had a great sorrow. (**Teacher:** Read verse 2.) Paul was a Jew. (See Acts 21:39.) He was thinking of the multitudes of Jews who had not received the Lord Jesus as Saviour. He wished with all his heart that there was something he could do to save them from eternal death. He had taught them that God condemns and punishes sin. He had explained that God would forgive their sins and count them righteous and sanctified if they would place their trust in the Lord Jesus Christ. But they had refused to believe his message. This was the reason for his sorrow. He knew that these Jews would be forever separated from God. He wrote, "I could wish that I myself could be cut off from Christ if my fellow Jews would be won for God." (See Romans 9:3.) But Paul knew that was not possible. No one can receive God's gift of salvation for another. Each must make this decision himself/herself. And each must accept the results of this decision–either salvation or damnation.

It was especially unfortunate that the Jewish people, the Israelites, refused God's gift of salvation. God had chosen this nation as His own special treasure (see Psalm 135:4) to receive His love and unusual blessing. (See Isaiah 43.)

Hundreds of years before Paul wrote the letter to the Romans, God said to Abraham, "I will bless you, and will multiply your children as the stars in Heaven and as the sand on the seashore." (See Genesis 22:17.) God chose Abraham to be the father of the great nation Israel. Why God chose the Israelites we are not told. But because He is God, He has the right to do what He wants to do. (See Deuteronomy 7:6-8.)

In Romans 9:4-5, Paul lists seven blessings that God gave only to Israel. Each was an evidence of God's special love for them. You will want to list these in your notebook.

## 1. GOD 'ADOPTED' ISRAEL AS A SON
### Exodus 4:22; Romans 9:4

### Show Illustration #1A

God said, "Israel is My son, even My first-born." (See Exodus 4:22.) God considered the nation of Israel as His son. What does a good father do for his son? He loves him, feeds and clothes him, and protects him. This is exactly how God cared for the Israelites. He loved them, provided for their needs and protected them. In yet another way God provided for the Jews: He punished them for their disobedience. Every loving father knows that he must punish his children when they do wrong. Although it makes a father unhappy to punish his children, he does so because he loves them and wants what is best for them.

The Israelites didn't always understand what was best for them. Sometimes they refused to listen to God and did what they themselves thought was best. Then God had to allow some punishment to come to them so they would turn back to Him.

Once God permitted the Israelites to go to Egypt where they became slaves. They were treated cruelly by the Egyptians, and their lives were very hard. But God loved them and cared for them. He gave them a leader, Moses, who went to the king of Egypt and asked that the Israelites be set free. The king was stubborn and refused again and again. Each time he refused God sent more trouble to the Egyptians, until finally the king said, "Yes! Get out of my land." (See Exodus 12:31-32.)

God protected His people on their long journey from the land of Egypt into the land which He had promised to them. He kept them from harm when the Egyptians raced after them, trying to recapture them.

During the daytime when the Israelites marched toward their new land, God went before them in a large cloud. They couldn't see God Himself, but the cloud reminded them that He was with them. They didn't get lost on their journey, for God led the way and they followed Him. At night the cloud became fire, glowing brightly. So the Israelites were reminded that God was with them through the night. (See Numbers 9:16-23.)

Tenderly God cared for His people, giving them water to drink and food to eat. And when that long, long journey of 40 years (see Numbers 14:33-34) was ended, their clothing and shoes were not worn out. (See Deuteronomy 29:5; Psalm 105:39-45.) Why? Because God was taking care of His chosen people, Israel, as a father cares for his child. God said, "When Israel was a child, then I loved him, and called my son out of Egypt." (See Hosea 11:1.)

So one of God's blessings to the nation of Israel was adoption.

## 2. GOD'S GLORY–HIS PRESENCE AND POWER–WERE WITH ISRAEL
### Romans 9:4

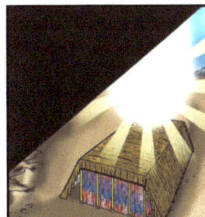

### Show Illustration #1B

During their 40-year journey to their homeland, God's people needed a movable place of worship. So God instructed Moses to build a tabernacle. God's glory rested over the tabernacle, reminding His people of His presence and power. The Israelites were blessed indeed.

## 3. GOD MADE COVENANTS (AGREEMENTS) WITH ISRAEL
### Romans 9:4

### Show Illustration #2A

God spoke to certain leaders of Israel giving promises to them and making agreements with them. No other nation ever received such covenants from God. (See Genesis 12:1-3; Galatians 3:6-9, 13-14.)

## 4. GOD GAVE HIS LAW TO ISRAEL
### Romans 9:4

### Show Illustration #2B

Israel received the words of God from His own hand. We have the Bible today because it was first given to the Jewish people. The Law was one more demonstration of God's special love for His people.

## 5. GOD GAVE THE ISRAELITES A SPECIAL SERVICE OF WORSHIP
### Romans 9:4

God entrusted to His dearly loved people a special service of marvelous meaning. In the tabernacle worship (and later in the temple) all their sacrifices and the service which they did were pictures of the Lord Jesus who was to come.

### Show Illustration #3A

Part of their service made it possible for them to have their sins covered.

In obedience to God they killed an

animal and sprinkled its blood on the altar. This was a picture of Jesus Christ, the Lamb of God, who would die for the world. God accepted their animal sacrifices as a substitute during the years before the sacrifice of His own Son. To have their sins covered was indeed a wonderful privilege.

## 6. GOD GAVE THE ISRAELITES HIS PROMISES
Romans 9:4

### Show Illustration #3B

Hundreds of years before Paul lived, God's prophets wrote His promises of blessings that would come to the Jews. Those promises will be fulfilled in the future when the Lord Jesus reigns as King over the earth. At that time the Jewish people will recognize Him as God the Son. Yes, God loved the Jewish nation dearly and made promises to them.

## 7. GOD GAVE THE ISRAELITES FATHERS (ANCESTORS)
Romans 9:5

### Show Illustration #4

Jews can trace their ancestry back to men who lived several thousand years ago–Abraham, Isaac, Jacob. Best of all blessings was that from those same "fathers" came the Lord Jesus Christ. He was born of a virgin–a real Man in a true body of flesh and blood. But at the same time He was, and is, God.

Even though God blessed the nation of Israel with so many wonderful blessings, they refused to receive the Saviour. Indeed, their religious and political leaders hated Him and had Him nailed to a cross. (The Gentiles were no better. It was a Roman governor who sentenced Him and Roman soldiers who crucified Him.) The Jews thought it was enough to obey certain laws of God rather than to have faith in the Lord Jesus Christ. (See Romans 9:32.) But the love of God never ends. Because He is righteous, His salvation is still offered to Israel– and to us. He invites Jews and Gentiles to do exactly the same thing: to place their trust in Jesus Christ. Are you trusting in Him? Remember: "Whosoever shall call upon the name of the Lord shall be saved." You can call upon Him and receive Him this moment.

> **NOTE TO THE TEACHER**
>
> Using the questions which appear in the beginning of lesson #2, have your students write the questions and answers in their notebooks.

# Lesson 2
# ISRAEL IN THE PRESENT

> **NOTE TO THE TEACHER**
>
> Romans 9, 10 and 11 contain a warning for us. Here we learn that God set aside Israel, the nation. The Israelites had been objects of His special blessing. However, they thought that if they kept the law reasonably well, this was enough to make them acceptable to God. They didn't realize that no one can keep the law perfectly. And if even one law is broken, the one who breaks it is guilty of breaking all the law. (See James 2:10.) That is why God demanded that animals be sacrificed for sins. Today, as when Paul wrote to the Romans, God requires faith in His Son, the Lord Jesus Christ, the Lamb of God who died for the sin of the world. But Israel refused what God required. As punishment for the sins of His chosen people, He has scattered them throughout the world.
>
> Hundreds of years ago, after their enemies had driven them out of their own land, some Jews settled in Germany. It was not very long until their troubles began there also. They were killed by the hundreds and their homes were destroyed. Those who were able to escape fled to England, expecting that the king would be kind and protect them. But again they suffered. They were robbed and thrown into prison. Whenever anything went wrong, the Jews were blamed and killed. Finally the king ordered all the Jews to leave his country.
>
> Later the Jewish people fled to France. There they were falsely accused of killing Christian children. The king put them in jail and forced them to pay large amounts of money to be freed. Before long a terrible sickness swept through the country and hundreds of people died. Again the Jews were blamed. "These people have poisoned our wells and streams," their enemies said. And once again the Jewish people were killed by the hundreds.
>
> From one country to another the Jews fled, trying to find a place of safety. Just as God had said, they were being scattered into every country in the world. In most places their possessions were stolen, their houses and synagogues were destroyed, and many were killed by their enemies.
>
> The Jews fled from Poland to Spain, and from Turkey to Russia. Hundreds of years passed. Still they suffered. In the 1940's six million Jews were killed by one dictator (Hitler). The tragic thing is that the Lord Jesus had said, "I would have gathered you as a hen gathers her chicks under her wings." But they would not hear Him.

**Scripture to be studied:** Romans 10

**The *aim* of the lesson:** To show your students how serious it is to reject the Lord Jesus Christ.

  **What your students should *know*:** God loves them, just as He loves the Jews, and wants them to be saved from sin.

  **What your students should *feel*:** A desire to be saved.

  **What your students should *do*:** Believe that Jesus is Lord, that God raised Him from the dead, and receive Him as Saviour.

**Lesson outline (for the teacher's and students' notebooks):**

  1. Jesus offered His love to Israel and cried when the people rejected Him (Matthew 23:37-39).

2. Because Israel refused ro receive the Lord Jesus, the Jews are spiritually blinded (Romans 11:25b).

3. Because the Israelites rejected His Son, God turned away from them (Matthew 21:33-46).

4. God continues to offer salvation to Israel (Romans 10:21).

**The verse to be memorized:**

*For whosoever shall call upon the name of the Lord shall be saved.* (Romans 10:13)

## REVIEW QUESTIONS

1. What nation is known as God's chosen people? *(Israel)*

2. The Israelites are known by what other names? *(Jews, Hebrews)*

3. What seven blessings did God give to the nation Israel? *(Adoption, Glory, Covenants, Law, Service, Promises, Fathers)*

4. What is meant by each of these blessings? *(Use the illustrations in the first lesson to help your pupils with the answer to this question. Review carefully.)*

5. Did Israel receive God's promised Saviour? *(No, they rejected Him and sent Him to death.)*

Will you please write in your notebook:

**B. God and Israel in the Present**
Romans 10
Israel Rejected

(*Teacher:* At the end of today's lesson, students should write what Israel must do to be saved from the penalty of sin. Take time to check their answers to be certain that what they have written is correct.)

## THE LESSON

What made the Apostle Paul sorrowful at the time he wrote Romans 9 and 10? Because the nation of Israel had rejected Jesus. Therefore, they would be forever separated from God. Paul said that the great desire of his heart and his prayer to God for Israel was that they might be saved. He knew that the Israelites wanted to have their sins forgiven. They wanted to be declared righteous before God. But they made the mistake of supposing that, because they tried to keep His law, that was enough. They would not accept God's way. They refused to place their trust in Jesus as Saviour. (See Romans 10:1-3.)

So this nation, which God loved so dearly and which He had blessed in such special ways, suffered punishment. God said they could no longer live in their homeland–the land into which He had led them from Egypt. They would be cut off from it because they had turned away from Him. (See 1 Kings 9:7.) They would no longer be recognized as a nation, but would be scattered among other nations of the world. (See Deuteronomy 4:27.) God would no longer protect them and fight against their enemies, as He had done before. Instead they would be hated and tormented by their enemies. They would not have rest, but would have fear and sorrow. Their lives would be in danger, and many would be killed. (See Deuteronomy 28:63-67.) And that is exactly what has happened. God's chosen people, the ones He had called His own, have been severely punished. Why? Because they wanted God to receive them because of their good works. But God wanted them to receive His Son.

## 1. JESUS OFFERED HIS LOVE TO ISRAEL AND CRIED WHEN THE PEOPLE REJECTED HIM
**Matthew 23:37-39**

The Lord Jesus showed His sorrow also when the Israelites refused His offer of love and forgiveness.

### Show Illustration #5

He cried, saying, "O Israel! I want to love you and gather you to Myself, just as a hen gathers her chicks under her wings; but you would not. Now you will know days of punishment and evil times . . . ." (See Matthew 23:37-39; Luke 13:34-35.) (Do you see in the illustration how the little chicks are refusing to come to the mother hen?)

Hundreds of years have passed since Jesus spoke those words. Israel has not yet accepted Him. Have the Jews known punishment and evil times as Jesus said? Yes, indeed. For all these centuries they have gone from country to country; in almost every place they have been hated. Many have been killed. Some have escaped to other lands, where they were not wanted.

While many are still wandering from place to place, thousands have today returned to their homeland, Israel. But even there they do not enjoy perfect peace. There is constant threat of war from their enemies. Why? Because they still refuse to place their trust in the Son of God.

## 2. BECAUSE ISRAEL REFUSED TO RECEIVE THE LORD JESUS, THE JEWS ARE SPIRITUALLY BLINDED
**Romans 11:25b**

As God foretold, Israel has been scattered and has suffered great trouble. Yet there is another punishment. The Israelites have been blinded. (See Romans 11:25b.) This doesn't mean that their eyes are blind so that they cannot see. Rather, it means that their minds and hearts are darkened so that they do not understand and believe in Christ Jesus. Have you ever had sore eyes? Perhaps during the night, while you slept, a crust formed on your eyelids and you weren't able to open your eyes in the morning. Your eyes weren't blind, but something kept you from seeing.

### Show Illustration #6

So it is with Israel. Their sin of rejecting the Lord Jesus Christ has blinded them so that they won't understand and put their trust in Him. Each time they hear of His love and refuse to receive Him, they become more blind.

Does this mean these Jews can never be saved? Oh, no! God has said that whoever calls upon the name of the Lord will be saved. "For there is no difference between the Jew and the Gentile: for the same Lord over all is rich unto all that call upon Him." (See

– 21 –

Romans 10:12-13.) God is eager to have His chosen people turn to Him. But most of them continually refuse Him.

The same sun that melts wax, also hardens clay. Did you ever take a piece of wax and place it in the hot sun? What happens to it? First it becomes soft and then it melts. But what happens to a piece of clay (or mud)? The longer it bakes in the sun, the harder it becomes. Sunbaked bricks are so hard that they can be used for building. Is the sun different? No. It's the material on which the sun beats that makes the difference. People are like this, too. Some hear the Gospel message of Jesus' love and are softened and place their trust in Him. Others, like so many Jews and Gentiles today, hear the same message, but by refusing it, become harder and harder.

## 3. BECAUSE THE ISRAELITES REJECTED HIS SON, GOD TURNED AWAY FROM THEM
Matthew 21:33-46

Jesus once told the Israelites a story about a man who planted a vineyard and hired some farmers to tend it for him. (See Matthew 21:33-46.) When it was time for the fruit to be gathered, the owner of the vineyard sent some of his servants to the farmers to get the fruit.

### Show Illustration #7

But the farmers took the servants and beat one, stoned another, and killed another. Again the owner sent servants to the farmers and the same thing happened. Then the owner sent his son, thinking that surely the farmers would respect his son more than they had respected his servants. But the farmers dragged the son from the vineyard and killed him!

When Jesus finished telling the story He asked, "When the owner of the vineyard comes, what will he do to those farmers?"

Quickly the Jews replied, "He will destroy those wicked men and will hire other farmers who will give him the fruit when it's ripe."

Then Jesus told His listeners that they were exactly like the wicked farmers. They wouldn't listen to the prophets, the servants of God who gave God's message to them. And when He Himself, the Son of God, came to them, they would not listen to Him either. Instead they planned how they could kill Him. So God turned away from Israel because they rejected His Son.

## 4. GOD CONTINUES TO OFFER HIS SALVATION TO ISRAEL
Romans 10:21

But wait! We must read the last verse of Romans 10. (*Teacher:* Read the verse, please.)

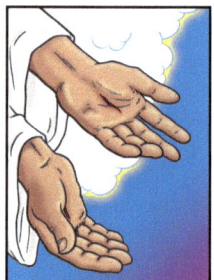

### Show Illustration #8

Today God still says to the Jewish nation, "All day long I have held out My hand to you who would not obey Me and who work against Me." (See also Isaiah 65:2.) God's chosen people have been rebellious. They have chosen their own way instead of God's way. But God still loves them. And because He is righteous, He continues to invite them to receive the Lord Jesus Christ.

God loves you, too. If you believe that Jesus is the Lord and that God raised Him from the dead, you will be saved from the penalty of sin, you will be made right with God. Then you will want to tell others how you have been saved from sin and its penalty. (*Teacher:* Read Romans 10:9-10.)

Remember! Whoever calls upon the name of the Lord will be saved. That message is the same for every Jew, for all who are not Jews, and it is for you.

---

### Lesson 3
# GOD AND ISRAEL IN THE FUTURE

### NOTE TO THE TEACHER

The righteousness of God: that is what the book of Romans is all about. And that righteousness shines clearly as we consider the future of Israel.

In Romans 9 we have seen how God's past dealings with Israel proved His righteousness in acting toward the Gentiles as He does now. In chapter 10 we have seen that although the nation Israel is presently set aside, this does not in any way forbid individual Israelites from turning to God and being saved. Paul is a marvelous example of the grace of God towards a Jew. What was true of him can be true of any other Israelite.

Israel (the nation) rejected every testimony sent to it. They rejected and killed the prophets and the Lord Jesus. So God rejects the nation, but he receives the individuals who believe in His Son.

Paul quotes from Isaiah in the Old Testament: "God hath given them the spirit of slumber, eyes that they should not see, and ears that they should not hear" (Isaiah 29:10). Then he quotes David: "Let their eyes be darkened, that they may not see" (Psalm 69:23).

The day came when the nation Israel deliberately rejected Christ and called for judgment to come to their descendants when they cried at the trial of Jesus, "His blood be upon us, and upon our children!" They rejected the Lord Jesus and God rejected them. Israel has "stumbled" (Romans 11:11). Israel has been temporarily "cast away" (Romans 11:15). Israel is "blinded in part" (Romans 11:25). But, as Paul proves, God is not through with the nation forever. A day is coming when a large number within Israel will turn back to God and to Christ whom they rejected. Then they will be a holy people and God's witnesses to all nations.

The future for the Jews is glorious. But before the glory there will be intense suffering and persecution. Many of them will die. If these are unsaved, they will be sent to the lake of fire forever. We must pray for the Jewish people and do all we can to get the Gospel to them–and to all others.

**Scripture to be studied:** Romans 11; 1 Kings 19:1-18; all verses mentioned in the text.

**The *aim* of the lesson:** To teach that while Israel suffers now because they reject Jesus Christ, they will one day receive Him and experience blessing.

**What your students should *know*:** God knows all that will happen to Israel and has future blessings for those who turn to Christ.

**What your students should *feel*:** A desire to know God and be a member of his family.

**What your students should *do*:** Believe on the Lord Jesus Christ and receive Him as Saviour.

**Lesson outline (for the teacher's and students' notebooks):**
1. Israel turned away from God to idols (Romans 11:1-10).
2. Because most Israelites rejected God's Son, God cut them off and offered salvation to the Gentiles (Romans 11:11-25).
3. The Israelites will return to their homeland (Deuteronomy 30:1-5).
4. One day, many Israelites will accept Jesus Christ as Saviour and King (Romans 11:26-27).

**The verse to be memorized:**

*For whosoever shall call upon the name of the Lord shall be saved.* (Romans 10:13)

## THE LESSON

We have studied about the past and present of the great nation of Israel. Today we shall learn of their future. Will you please write in your notebook:

### C. God and Israel in the Future
### Romans 11
### Israel's Reception

Have you ever been very unhappy? Did you think that you would never smile again? When we are feeling unhappy and see other people who seem happy, we think, "I will never feel that happy." It is hard to imagine that things will ever get better.

Suppose someone would say to you, "Don't worry. Things are bad today. But tomorrow will be different. All your worries and troubles will be over and you will be happy again!" If someone could make such a promise and it would really come true, it would be wonderful.

The Israelites are God's chosen people. Once they enjoyed His special blessings. Despite this, they turned away from Him. Then their troubles began. Because they turned away from God, God turned away from the nation Israel. He removed His protection from them and allowed them to suffer.

Part of Israel's suffering, you will remember, is blindness. As long as they continue to reject the Lord Jesus they won't understand God's purposes, and their hearts and wills hardened. They are like blind people who stumble in darkness.

This is truly a sad time for Israel. But the sadness will not last forever. God's Word promises that a better, happier time will come. And that could be soon.

One happy thought is that not all Jewish people are enemies of God. Our memory verse has been reminding us that everyone –either Jew or Gentile– who calls on the name of the Lord will be saved. Happily, there are some Jews who have believed in the Lord Jesus and are faithful to Him.

## 1. ISRAEL TURNED AWAY FROM GOD TO IDOLS
### Romans 11:1-10

In Romans chapter 11, Paul writes of something that had happened many hundreds of years before the Lord Jesus came to earth. The Israelites had disobeyed God and turned to worship a heathen idol, Baal.

### Show Illustration #9

King Ahab and his wicked queen, Jezebel, led the people in worshiping Baal. They killed many of the prophets who tried to preach God's message. The wicked Jezebel sent a message to a prophet of God, Elijah, saying, "Before this same time tomorrow you, too, will be dead!" (See 1 Kings 19:2.)

That made Elijah lose his courage. It seemed as if he was the only one who loved the Lord God. *No one else will listen to God's Word and obey His laws,* Elijah thought. He was tired, discouraged and afraid. So he ran to the mountains and hid in a cave. But he couldn't hide from God. The voice of God called, saying, "What are you doing here, Elijah?"

Sadly Elijah replied, "The children of Israel will not listen. They have disobeyed Your laws and thrown down Your altars. They have even killed the other prophets. I am the only one left. I am all alone. I am the only one in the whole nation who serves You, the true and living God. And now my life is in danger. They are hunting me to kill me!"

But God said, "Don't be afraid. Go back to your people and do what I tell you to do. You are not the only one who loves Me. I still have 7,000 people in Israel who have not bowed their knees to Baal."

That was good news! Elijah was not the only one who loved and served the living God. There were 7,000 more who hadn't turned against God to bow before the heathen god, Baal.

From the time of Elijah until now, there have always been some Israelites who have believed and have not turned away from God. (See Romans 11:5.) Even though God has had to reject Israel as a nation because of its unbelief, there will always be some individuals who truly believe. These God gladly receives as His own people.

## 2. BECAUSE MOST ISRAELITES REJECTED GOD'S SON, GOD CUT THEM OFF AND OFFERED SALVATION TO THE GENTILES
### Romans 11:11-25

Because Israel turned away from God, God commanded that His message of love should be given to the Gentile nations. So it is that men and women, and boys and girls, of almost every nation have heard and received the good news of salvation. Those who have believed in the Lord Jesus Christ and received Him as Saviour have been adopted into God's family.

We can understand this better if we think of the example of the olive tree, told by the Apostle Paul in Romans 11. Many hundreds of years ago. God made Abraham the father of the Jewish nation. He was the first Jew. From him and his children all the Israelites have come, just as branches grow on a tree. Abraham was the beginning, like the trunk of the tree, and more and more branches were added as the tree (the nation of Israel) grew. One day the Saviour, too, was born into this nation. But most of the Israelites rejected Him and God had to cut them off the tree.

### Show Illustration #10

A farmer prunes the diseased branches from a tree. Just so God had to remove the disobedient branches of Israelites.

What did God do then? He took other branches and grafted them into His olive tree where they could grow in place of the branches that had been trimmed away. Who are these "other branches"? They are Gentiles who have placed their trust in the Lord Jesus and received Him as Saviour. Because they have been born again, they are members of the family of God. Now Jewish believers and Gentile believers are all growing together.

Do Gentile believers have any reason to boast? Are they better than the Jews because they believe, whereas many Jews do not? No, indeed! The branches of a tree get their life from the roots. None of them can survive alone. Salvation for both Gentiles and Jews depends upon the love of God. Not one of us has any reason to boast. Today, both Jew and Gentile are saved the same way–through faith in the Lord Jesus Christ as Saviour.

## 3. THE ISRAELITES WILL RETURN TO THEIR HOMELAND
### Deuteronomy 30:1-5

But God's Word says that one day Israel will recognize the Lord Jesus as Saviour. (See Romans 11:26-27.) Then the disobedient branches which He broke off will be grafted back into the olive tree (Romans 11:24). What a wonderful day that will be when many in Israel will repent and be reunited to God through faith in the Lord Jesus Christ!

When will this day come? We do not know exactly. But God's Word tells us of events that will happen before that day. Some of them are happening even now. When God's Church (all believers, both Jew and Gentile) is complete, the Lord Jesus will take His own people to be with Him. (See 1 Thessalonians 4:13-18; 1 Corinthians 15:51-52.) And the Israelites who have been scattered throughout the world for hundreds of years will then be regathered into their own land. (See Isaiah 11:11-12.)

### Show Illustration #11

This is already beginning to happen. Other nations now recognize Israel as a nation again. Many Jewish people are returning to their homeland. Surely it cannot be too long before the Lord Jesus will come for His own. Then the last of the sorrowful times, which Israel has suffered for so long, will begin. This time of Great Tribulation will be worse than any of the other sufferings ever known by Israel. (See Matthew 24:21.) It will be a time of wickedness, fear, sorrow and danger. Yet during all that time, a small group of Jewish believers will be witnesses for the Lord. Because of their faithful witness, many people will repent and believe in Christ, receiving Him as Saviour. (See Revelation 7:3-17.)

## 4. ONE DAY, MANY ISRAELITES WILL ACCEPT JESUS CHRIST AS SAVIOUR AND KING
### Romans 11:26-27

### Show Illustration #12

Then, after seven years of tribulation are finally ended, the Lord Jesus Christ will return to earth as King. At that time Israel's blindness will be ended and they will understand God's goodness. A large number of them will receive the Lord Jesus as Saviour and will claim Him as their King. This is the wonderful day which God has promised. God's chosen people will enjoy His special blessings once more. They will understand God's love for them and worship Him as the true God. Their land will be blessed and will produce great harvests of food. (Study Isaiah 35.) They will enjoy the presence of Jesus as their King, seeing Him with their own eyes. They will no longer be hated by their enemies, for they will have no enemies. Instead, they will be honored because they are Jews. (See Zechariah 8:23.) Then the world will at last enjoy a time of peace and blessing. This is known as the Millennium.

What a glad day that will be! God, the righteous One, is the only One who could plan such blessings! Do you know Him? Are you a member of His family through faith in the Lord Jesus Christ? If not, you may receive Him this very moment.

---

### NOTE TO THE TEACHER

In Illustration #11, we have pictured Jews in clothing of Bible times returning to their homeland. However, they will doubtless wear the dress of whatever land they have been living in. We have used the kind of clothing that was worn in Bible times simply because we could not use all the kinds of clothes that will be worn. You will see on the map numbers instead of names of countries (as of 1971) and rivers. If you would like to enter the names they are as follows:

1. Lebanon
2. Syria
3. Israel
4. Jordan
5. Iraq
6. Saudi Arabia
7. Egypt
8. Euphrates River (We know this will be the eastern boundary of Israel in the future. See Genesis 15:18.)
9. Nile River
10. Wady El Arish (It is not certain if the western boundary will be the Nile River or the Wady El Arish.)
11. Red Sea

# Lesson 4
# ISRAEL–PAST, PRESENT AND FUTURE

## NOTE TO THE TEACHER

The Jews need to hear the Gospel. And they must hear it from us who have been born again. Even if you do not have Jewish people in your neighborhood, ask the Lord to show you how you can share the good news with them wherever they are. Be sure to pray for them.

As we have learned from Romans 11, spiritual blindness has come to Israel. God allowed this because they rejected His Son. Jews now make the great mistake of feeling that because they are Jewish, God accepts them. Romans 9:4-8 proves this is wrong. No Jewish person can claim that he is right with God just because he has descended from Abraham.

The Jews also make the mistake of thinking that salvation is by doing–that is, by keeping the law. (See Romans 9:31-32.) What Paul wrote in Romans 10:2-3 is just as true of Israel today, hundreds of years later. The Jewish people refuse to receive salvation and the righteousness of God by faith alone. They insist upon working for it.

However, if any Jew is going to be saved, he must be saved exactly the same way that anyone else is saved–by placing his trust in the Lord Jesus Christ. (See Romans 10:411:6.)

How can we meet the need of the Jews? We must love them. Read again in Romans 9:1-3, Paul's concern for the Jewish people. He cared so much for them that he could wish himself cut off from the Lord Jesus Christ in order to see them saved. That kind of feeling for people cannot be hidden. And people–whether Jew or Gentile–respond when you love them like that.

Pray that God will give you a genuine concern for the lost of your class, as well as for the lost all around you.

**Scripture to be studied:** Romans 11; Ezekiel 37:1-14.

**The *aim* of the lesson:** To teach that one day Israel will turn to God and claim Jesus Christ as Saviour.

**What your students should *know*:** Believers have the responsibility of taking the Gospel to the Jews.

**What your students should *feel*:** A desire to be a witness for God to the Jews.

**What your students should *do*:** Be a witness for God this week.

**Lesson outline (for the teacher's and students' notebooks):**

1. Ezekiel has a vision of dry bones (Israel scattered) (Ezekiel 37:1-2).
2. The dry bones come together (Israel will be regathered in its homeland) (Ezekiel 37:3-14).
3. God blessed the world through the Jews.
   A. The Jews were to be witnesses for God (Isaiah 43:10, 12).
   B. Israel was to preserve the Scriptures (Deuteronomy 4:5-8; Romans 3:2).
   C. The Saviour came from the Jewish nation (Micah 5:2).
4. Israel will one day turn to Jesus Christ (Romans 11:26-27).

**The verse to be memorized:**

*For whosoever shall call upon the name of the Lord shall be saved.* (Romans 10:13)

## THE LESSON

### 1. EZEKIEL HAS A VISION OF DRY BONES (ISRAEL SCATTERED)
#### Ezekiel 37:1-2

Many hundreds of years ago, God gave a vision to the prophet Ezekiel, to tell him what would happen one day to the nation Israel. In his vision, Ezekiel was led by the Spirit of God into a valley. No one else was there, and it was very quiet.

### Show Illustration #13

Looking around him, Ezekiel saw that the ground was covered with old, dry bones. He walked all around, back and forth across the valley. But everywhere he walked he saw only bones–hundreds of them. They had lain on the ground under the hot sun for a long time. So the bones were white and dry and brittle.

God asked Ezekiel, "Can these bones live?"

Ezekiel probably thought for a moment before answering. He may have wondered, *How could these bones possibly live again? The flesh has been gone for many years. Even if someone could find the bones which belong together, how could they ever be changed into living, breathing men?* But Ezekiel knew that all things are possible with God. God had created the first man, Adam, from the dust of the earth. Surely He could bring dry bones to life again. To God's question, "Can these bones live?" Ezekiel answered, "O Lord God, You know."

### 2. THE DRY BONES COME TOGETHER (ISRAEL WILL BE REGATHERED IN ITS HOMELAND)
#### Ezekiel 37:3-14

Then God commanded Ezekiel to speak to the bones, telling them that He would perform a miracle–He would bring the bones to life!

Ezekiel did exactly as the Lord had commanded. And a strange thing took place! In his vision, Ezekiel heard a rattling noise. The bones were beginning to move.

### Show Illustration #14

Each bone seemed to be seeking a partner and joining itself to other bones. There were the bones for an arm, and there were the bones for a leg. As Ezekiel watched, flesh covered the bones. Then skin covered flesh. Finally they were no longer dry bones. They were people! But they were not moving. There was no breath in them. Then God caused the wind to blow across the valley and breathe into each body. The motionless people began to move. One after another, they opened their eyes and stood to their feet. Where once there had been a valley full of dry bones, there was now a huge crowd of living, breathing people.

What did the strange vision mean? God explained it to Ezekiel, saying, "These bones are the nation of Israel. Right now the Israelites are like dead, scattered bones. They have been scattered throughout the whole world. But one day I will gather these scattered ones together in their own land." And God promised, "I will put My spirit in you, Israel, and you shall live. And I will place you in your own land. Then will you know that I, the Lord, have spoken it and performed it." What a wonderful promise!

How had Israel become as dead, dry bones? At one time they had enjoyed God's wonderful blessings. But they turned their backs on God. So God rejected them–but not forever, as we saw in our last lesson.

# 3. GOD BLESSED THE WORLD THROUGH THE JEWS

God chose the Jews for His own special people. He wanted the rest of the world to be blessed through them in three ways. (You will want to write these in your notebook.)

### A. The Jews Were to be Witnesses for God
### Isaiah 43:10, 12

## Show Illustration #15

The first Israelites had wicked neighbors who knew nothing about the living God. They worshiped idols that could not see or hear, that could not answer their prayers. Many of these people did dreadful things to try to please their false gods. Some of them even killed their own children and offered them as sacrifices to their idols. God wanted His chosen people to tell their neighbors about Him. He wanted these idol worshipers to know from His Word that He is the one true and living God, and that He is the God of love and mercy and power.

Sometimes the Israelites were obedient to God, so that some of their neighbors did turn to the worship of the true God of Heaven. But many times the Israelites turned away from God and worshiped the idols, just as the nations around them did. Often, as in Elijah's time, the Israelites built altars to the heathen gods. They refused to listen to the prophets who tried to warn them of their wickedness. Instead of listening and repenting of their sins, they killed the prophets. What a pity, since God wanted to bless the rest of the world through the witness of His people.

God wanted to bless the world in another way:

### B. Israel Was to Preserve the Scriptures
### Deuteronomy 4:5-8; Romans 3:2

## Show Illustration #16A

God intended that the Israelites should carefully guard His holy Word (written at that time on scrolls) and teach it faithfully to their children. Nothing should be added to the Word of God and nothing was to be taken from it, so that, year after year, God's Word would be the same. Throughout all the years of time, God wanted people to be able to read and understand His way of salvation, as written in the holy Scriptures.

Strangely enough, although the nation of Israel rejected God's way of salvation through the Lord Jesus Christ, they have been very careful to preserve His written Word. Several years ago, a certain Jewish congregation discovered that one of their holy scrolls was missing. They searched carefully throughout their synagogue, then began searching outside. Someone must have stolen the scroll, which contained part of the Scriptures. Finally the missing scroll was found, but it had been partly burned. So great was their grief that they held a funeral service for the scroll. It was tenderly wrapped in a shawl and buried in a wooden box. Then the whole congregation mourned for one week. Yes, the Israelites do love and guard the Scriptures. But they don't understand what the Scriptures teach concerning the Lord Jesus Christ.

### C. The Saviour Came from the Jewish Nation
### Micah 5:2

## Show Illustration #16B

Matthew spoke of Jesus as the son of David, the son of Abraham. God's promise to Abraham, made long ago, was fulfilled. God had said that all the nations of the earth would be blessed through the family of Abraham. And the Lord Jesus, God's own Son, was born into that family.

How much Israel was blessed! How much they could have enjoyed! They were chosen by God for these very special honors: (1) They were to be the messengers to the world of the one true and living God of Heaven. (2) They were given the privilege of receiving and caring for the written Word of the living God. (3) They were especially honored by being the nation chosen to bring forth the Saviour of the world. What could be more wonderful?

But Israel rejected God and because of this rejection, has suffered much. Has God been too hard on Israel? Oh, no. God is too good to be unkind and too wise to make mistakes. He the righteous One loves Israel. His judgments have been for the purpose of showing mercy to those who would believe in His Son. God offers His love and forgiveness to all. Sometimes He allows trouble to come, to remind people of their need of Him.

The world today is like a super jet flying swiftly on course. Satan is the captain and is steering the plane toward certain destruction. Those on board do not see any danger. They seem to be having a good time, enjoying sin and ignoring God. But now God allows a storm to come. And as the plane heaves up and down in the turbulence, some of the people on board are brought to their senses. They see their need of the Saviour and they turn to God for forgiveness of sin. God's purpose in allowing the storm has been to save those who would turn to Him.

# 4. ISRAEL WILL ONE DAY TURN TO JESUS CHRIST
### Romans 11:26-27

One future day Israel, too, will turn to God and will claim the Lord Jesus as Saviour. When Jesus came to earth the first time, it was to die on the cross.

## Show Illustration #12

The next time He comes to earth He, the King, will sit on His throne. Israel treated the Lord shamefully at His first coming. But when He comes as King to rule a thousand years (Revelation 20:4), Israel will acknowledge Him as Lord and Saviour and bow in worship before Him (Philippians 2:10-11).

Has God forgotten Israel? Never. The Apostle Paul reminds us that "the gifts and calling of God are without repentance." (See Romans 11:29.) God never takes back the gifts He has given. He doesn't change His mind about those to whom He gives His grace. One day Israel will receive full blessing from God.

Do believers have any responsibility toward Jewish people today? Yes. Those who believe in Christ as their Saviour should love the Jews, for they are God's chosen people. Every true follower of the Lord Jesus should be doing whatever he/she can to give the Gospel message to Jews. Remember, the Apostle said that the Gospel of Christ is the power of God unto salvation, to everyone who believes–to the Jew first, and also to the Gentile. (See Romans 1:16.) Who can fully understand the mercy and righteousness and love of God?

Do you have your faith in His Son? Remember! Whoever (and that includes you!) calls on the name of the Lord Jesus Christ, will be saved.

www.ingramcontent.com/pod-product-compliance
Lightning Source LLC
Chambersburg PA
CBHW060804090426
42736CB00002B/147